THE MEKONG DRAGON

Lily H. Trieu

THE MEKONG DRAGON

© 2023, Lily H. Trieu.

All rights reserved. This book or any portion thereof may not be reproduced or used in any manner whatsoever without the express written permission of the publisher except for the use of brief quotations in a book review.

First Edition

Print ISBN: 979-8-35093-149-5
eBook ISBN: 979-8-35093-150-1

CONTENTS

Preface i

Dedication v

Chapter 1: Living With the Unknowns 1

Chapter 2: The Waiting Game 15

Chapter 3: New Home, New Land 25

Chapter 4: Starting Over 35

Chapter 5: Heartache 41

Chapter 6: The Love of My Life 49

Chapter 7: Continuing the Legacy: The Next Generation ... 56

Chapter 8: My Family 62

Epilogue 71

Lily's Closing Prayer 73

Favorite Vietnamese Recipes 77

Preface

While this story may sound like just another immigrant's story of coming to America, "Land of Opportunity" and new beginnings, of hardships, hard work, resilience, determination, and a commitment to family, it is much more. It is a journey of love, grace, relationships, and hope. This is my faith journey.

My mother was a devout Catholic. I was not. Neither was I a Buddhist. We believed in a religion of ancestor worship; that those who have died continue to exist and still have the ability to influence the fates of those who are living. That is why we celebrate New Year's and anniversaries of their death by burning incense and inviting them to come back into the house to protect us. We go to the pagoda once a year unlike devout Catholics who go to church regularly on Sunday. I dismissed my mother's Catholicism as unimportant. I never attended Mass with her; I never questioned her with the intention of learning more; it was *her* thing. And I was not going to abandon what I believed.

When Dinh and I came to Greenville, TX, we were one of the first Vietnamese families to arrive. After the war, more and more families came to build a new life, and as is the immigrant-way, we created our own Asian community within Dallas. Asian communities are like any other. We have similar culture, language, and traditions. But Vietnamese are diverse in their religious beliefs, and like my mother, many Catholics "got off the boat." We worshiped our ancestors for seventy-five years, and I don't know why on his death-bed, Dinh wanted to become a Catholic as he was about to take his last breath. That night, he accepted Jesus as his Lord and Savior. This priest who officiated over this conversion was a priest from Vietnam visiting the Mother of Perpetual Help Parish in Garland, TX. At Dinh's funeral, this congregation celebrated his life with songs, prayers, and a beautiful funeral Mass and love to our family. That was the real beginning of my journey. This church family's actions spoke of Jesus' and God's love and caring. They embraced me, taught me, accepted me, and supported me as I mourned the great love of my life. I was beginning to think my guy had done the right thing. Today, I am a baptized and an active member of Mother of Perpetual Help Parish, and for me, it is well named. They were the wellspring of my hope for a new life. My faith is the foundation of my life, and I celebrate everyday all of God's blessings with joy and humility.

I would like to thank a few of those blessings; God for his love and the congregation of my church for accepting me. My love, my husband, my best friend: Dinh. Throughout my life, I never had to worry about how things were going to work out because I knew Dinh would manage. He would know how to get this family on a boat out of Saigon, and out of harm's way. We were lucky that Dinh found the way to help us leave Saigon while so many people were forced to stay behind and suffer through the war. I knew he was not going to be a custodian for very long as this was just his first job in this "Land of Opportunity," not his last. I knew he would figure out a way to support his family to thrive and succeed. And in the end, I learned he would lead the way for me to find peace, love, and faith after his death. Now I know he watches over me. My love for him is without measure.

My mother: Dung. My mother raised me with unconditional love. She dedicated her life to me and all her children. She would go to bed hungry just to be sure her children were fed. I would like to dedicate my success to my mother and all her sacrifices and lessons that showed me the way to live my life.

My children: Tama, Ty, Le, and Justine. I see the gifts of their heritage in each one of them. They have the inner strength of their ancestors and represent the best of where they came, and still each one carries their own unique American spirit.

Our Sponsors: Rev. Dan Shaw and his wife, Betsy, and Dr. Truett Crim and his wife, Margaret. These four supported and guided us from the first time they met us at the airport. They were our safety blanket and then our launching pad. We could not have made the transition so smoothly without them.

My English teacher: Susan Pokorski was an English teacher and School Principal for over twenty years. She holds a Bachelor of Arts Degree in English and Master's Degree in Education Leadership. She has been my English teacher since her son, Chaz, married my youngest daughter, Justine. She is so sweet and I love her like a sister.

Susan recalls, "I remember the warm welcome Dinh and Lily greeted their guests at our children's wedding. Both Dinh and Lily welcomed them in English and Vietnamese—which was not a surprise. But to my surprise, they then greeted us in French as well. What I didn't realize was that because many of Lily and Dinh's friends and family had immigrated to France before the Vietnam War, many of the guests that night had traveled from Paris to attend the wedding. Like the Vietnamese and English welcome, the French welcome was just as perfectly spoken. This was the just the first of many times that this couple has shown their level of accomplishments—their depth and breadth of understanding and thriving in the world around them. Working with Lily to capture some of the nuances of the English language has been a delight."

Dedication

As of this writing, it will be forty-seven years since we left our homeland of Vietnam. I have not forgotten my birthplace, and my hope is that future generations will be able to know, understand, and appreciate their heritage. I am writing and dedicating this book to my children and all their children.

CHAPTER ONE

Living With the Unknowns

My life has been rich with many blessings, the first of whom was my most amazing and resilient mother. My mother could turn a challenge into a miracle, a roving rogue into the love of her life, and scandal into "the high road." My mother lived a full bountiful life, and she died in 2005 at the age of ninety. And still my mother lives within me. Every day, I am driven by her actions, her beliefs, her love, and her never-ending courage.

At the time of her birth, Vietnam was a French colony called French Indochina. Life under colonialism for many of the Vietnamese people was very hard. The working-class people were called "coolies," a disrespectful term for Asian laborers. They worked long hours of physical toil with minimal wages. Many were paid in rice rather than money. My mother, Luu Thi Dung was born in Can Tho, Vietnam, the tenth child of eleven children. Can Tho is among the largest cities within the region of the Mekong Delta. The children neither did go to school nor did they have any shoes to wear. Every day, the children took care of the buffalo herd from the neighboring rice field's owner to make money to pay for their daily rice. Dung's family was victim of the system of French colonization that led to widespread misery among the peasants throughout Vietnam. As Dung's family was poor and could not support all the children, at eighteen years old, she followed her aunt to work as a seamstress in Saigon. She was a beautiful, young girl who was ready to take on the world as best she could. She worked for a tailor who was married with a family of his own. He became smitten with this young beauty. The tailor's wife realized what was taking place, and being worried that this could grow into something that would threaten her marriage, her family, and her future, she decided to take matters into her own hand. She was not going to allow this new young stranger to threaten her family. And as any jealous and terrified wife would do, the tailor's wife convinced her husband to introduce my mom to one of their customers, Trieu Van Yen.

Yen was a tall, handsome, "ladies' man" who came from a wealthy influential family in Saigon. He had studied in France and had a "French air" about him. His charm was irresistible. He was thirty-six years old. Dung was immediately attracted to him, and the attraction was returned. This beautiful couple began seeing each other. And soon, Dung was in love. Unbeknownst to her, Yen was also married with several children of his own. Soon, Dung discovered she was pregnant. Jealousy is a powerful and destructive emotion. The tailor's wife was a good and decent woman, but her jealousy led to the demise of a young girl and her future. When the tailor's wife found out that Dung was pregnant, she took this opportunity to kick her out with no money and no place to live in the big city of Saigon. The tailor couldn't interfere because his wife was so jealous of Dung. She knew that her husband had a crush on Dung. My mother had to deliver her baby (my elder brother) in a barn with only the help of a kind-hearted midwife.

This secret was only found out years later after my mother died. My sister-in-law, living in Paris, France, came to her funeral and told me. My mother had kept her secret for so long and never told me of the drama; she was afraid that if Dinh found out, he would have told his family of her misfortune. (Dinh's father was a well-known General Attorney at the Supreme Court and would have been ashamed of this very poor country girl who had a baby out of marriage.)

The tailor knew what they had done to Dung was terribly wrong, and he felt horrible about how his family had set her up with this rogue. Unable to live with this guilt and sense of wrongdoing, he took his own life. After the death of her husband, the tailor's wife couldn't take care of the business. She felt guilty and depressed and had a heart attack leaving five young orphans. Neither could rid themselves of the remorse of their actions and the impact it had had on their young employee's life.

Again, I do not know how Dung found out about the deaths, but once she heard the news, she went back to the five young orphans and took them under her wing. There were no others to care for them. She carried on with the business as well as she cared for, loved, and nurtured her now six children. She was not yet twenty years old. She had occasional suitors, but none could compare to the father of her child. She focused on working and caring for her family.

The second pregnancy from this relationship was me. Mother decided that even though many of the tailor's children had grown and were starting their own new lives by this time, she was not ready to have another child. With special herbs and tonics, she tried to induce an abortion. Me, being the most stubborn of all her children, was not ready to give up my unborn life and came into the world as scheduled. (I was the one who had the good fortune of sharing my own family with her as she graciously enjoyed her senior years.) She next had two more children, but they both died later of the influenza. My younger sister Lang was the next in line. She became a flight attendant for Air Vietnam and was later killed in an airplane crash where she was working. My younger brother Sang was the sixth child, and the baby of the crew was my sister, Nga Klein. I was eleven years old when she was born.

Yen would come and go into her life, and as unconventional a relationship as it was, it worked for my mother, for a while. She grew the business each year; she eventually bought and ran a tea/coffee plantation in Bao Loc, a city in Lam Dong in the central highlands of Vietnam. Bao Loc is famous for it registered trademark, B'lao tea, famous all over the world. She planned the crops, hired, and supervised the workers, as well as managed the business end.

As mother was making a life for herself and her family, Yen was traveling back and forth from Vietnam to France. He had found himself another girlfriend and set up this new "lover" in an apartment in Paris. My brother, Luu, had left for France before he finished high school. Mother knew that was the best place for him to make his fortune. Her dream was to send him to college in France after finishing high school there. Knowing that it would break her heart to send him to a foreign country so far away, she had to do it for pride and his safety. By the time the war eventually broke out, he would be out of the country and safe from the draft. She gave him what she could, but he started out with very little money. He was washing dishes at the time of his father's new affair.

He had kept up with his father, and when he found out about the girlfriend and the apartment, he wanted to take the apartment from her so he would have a better place to live. Yen tried to kick out his girlfriend for his son to move in. The girlfriend fought back and claimed that as she was living there, the apartment was hers. Yen sued her for it and unexpectedly won. Luu quickly moved in and began a new life for himself.

Yen returned to my mother. Mother always loved her man but by this time was fed up with his comings and goings into her life. At that point, she issued an ultimatum that he must marry her. They went to Blao (Bao Loc) and got a 2nd Degree of Marriage. This enabled Yen to remain married to his first wife, but under Vietnamese law, could take a "2nd Degree wife." We all changed our names and took Yen's last name. This would enable us to attend private schools later on. My mother had already set her standards high for her remaining children and their education.

Dung and Yen cohabitated as husband and wife living together and considered each other, husband and wife. Yen stayed with Dung until his death at seventy years old. Yen died before the war started.

Occasionally, we spent summers on the plantation. As the Americans entered the city, my mother bought and refurbished an old building that provided housing for those troops. She was a visionary, an entrepreneur, and a woman who valued and thrived in an ever-changing world.

Because we were a French colony, the French language was the first language in all the best schools. We would be sure to be proficient in both French and Vietnamese. We knew a little English. I started school from kindergarten at The Lycee Marie Curie, a very prestigious school in Saigon that only accepted the very wealthy and connected families from Saigon's "High Society." My father had the social standing and wealth to assure that I would be accepted. My father added my name as "Josephine," the name of Napoleon's wife. He thought it would be easier for the professors to pronounce. I was very fluent in French. My father knew Madame Caubet, Principal of the Lycee Marie, very well, and she let me tutor young students at school during summer time.

The measure of success was also to go to France and make your fortune. My mother made sure that her sons could succeed there. At sixteen years old, Luu had been sent to France with nothing but change in his pockets. He arrived with just a dream and a job as a dishwasher. Later, he became a very successful engineer and resided on the French Riviera. He was an excellent tennis player which lead him to the professional world of tennis. He became a regular umpire at the French Open. (My father had served as a tennis umpire all over the world as well, including the Olympics.)

When my daughter Justine and her family traveled to France years later, they visited Luu and his wife Clary. While enjoying a mid-day Mediterranean lunch on the French Riviera, Uncle Luu umpiring at the French Open, Justine asked Uncle Luu about his times umpiring. He laughed and said, "Well, there were many exciting games at the French Open, but probably the best thing I got from it was that there isn't anyone in the world who can now 'rattle' me by yelling at me—after all, I have been yelled at by the best." John McEnroe and Jimmy Connors topped the list. (Mr McEnroe and Mr Connors were two of the most aggressive umpire challengers of the times.)

My younger brother Sang followed in Luu's footsteps when he turned sixteen. Mother had become very successful by then so Sang landed in Paris with more than a little "change" in his pockets, and mother continued to support him as she could. Even with mother's support, he could not afford college in France. He went to Switzerland to study for his degree. He lived with several other Vietnamese students also studying in Switzerland. There he met a young student who would become his wife. The day they married, her family threw a celebration in Saigon, in order to honor and recognize the new family member. We happily attended that wonderful celebration. We wanted them to know how happy we were to welcome her and her family into ours. The young couple moved back to Paris after graduation and had very successful careers and family. Their daughter became a nuclear engineer and is world renown. She was offered one time a job with a computer company out of Beijing but turned them down. My mother was always proud of their success.

My baby sister Nga went to the United States as an Exchange Student in 1969 in Connecticut. In 1972, she obtained a full ride scholarship to attend a college in Virginia and graduated in 1975. She was in the United States when Saigon fell. After graduation, she married and settled in Florida with her husband. They have two children and four grandchildren.

In the late 1920s, the first group of Vietnamese began to challenge French rule. These were well educated Vietnamese who had lived in Europe. They had gained a better understanding of freedom, learning about democracy as well as communism. The most influential of these was the Indochinese Communist Party. Ho Chi Minh was the first leader to work to gain Vietnamese independence.

The wealth and power remained with the French and the wealthy Vietnamese as they partnered to build Vietnam into a powerful industrial country. And the history became even more convoluted when France fell to Germany in the 1940s. The 1930s was the era of French trying to take back control of Vietnam. Their focus was on industrial improvements but with little regard to the well-being of the Vietnamese people with whom Germany and Japan were allies, and when France fell, Japan took over many of the improvements France had worked to build including railroads, harbors, and airfields.

All of this was happening as Dung was raising a family and growing her businesses. She kept her focus on what she could control—her children, their safety, and their futures.

While she was not a graduate of any Business School, she was an intelligent and self-taught businesswomen with an intuitive ability to develop and grow many business ventures amid all the political turmoil. With her leading the way, our family was safe, well-educated, and loved.

In 1954, The Geneva Conference met and ended the French colonial presence in Vietnam. A partition was established that separated Vietnam into two states at the 17th parallel (The Demilitarized Zone.) The north was called the Democratic Republic of Vietnam and the south, The Republic of Vietnam. Communism had taken over Northern Vietnam. Over a million people left North Vietnam to escape communism. This exodus was called Operation Passage to Freedom. The Accord allowed for a 300-day grace period that allowed for people to move freely between the two states before the boundaries were sealed. Between 600 and 1,000,000 people moved to the south to escape communism. Many of these were Catholic. These pilgrims sought independence, freedom, and safety from anarchy. This movement was facilitated mainly by the French Air Force and Navy. American naval ships supplemented both the exodus and humanitarian relief once the refugees arrived in Saigon. As the new arrivals settled into their new home, Saigon then became the city of upper-class northerners and long-time residential southerners. The two did not mingle. The northerners thought of themselves to be more "cultured."

At that time, my father was very adamant that I stay away from "boys." However, a friend of mine, Julie, had introduced me to a young medical student who had his approval. Of course, my parents thought it would be a good match and would ensure an upper class standing and a stable future for me. My mother loved the medical student.

I liked him because he was a southerner, a smart and handsome guy. I went out with him a couple of times and was very interested. But later on, I found out that a lot of girls were also attracted to him. He was a big flirt and considered himself very hot. I was very shy, and like usual, I did not want to challenge. Feeling sad, I decided to quit seeing him. My mom always told me that he was a good catch and someone every mother would want for their daughter. Unfortunately, we have a saying in Vietnamese, "có duyên mà không có nợ," which means, "have grace without debt."

Two people may have a chance to fall in love but cannot stay together for certain other reasons. I broke up with him.

I was in eleventh grade, and I was still attending the Lycée Marie Curie, a prestigious all-girls school in Saigon. The new northern families did not mingle with the old southern families. They saw themselves as more upper class, more polished, and better educated.

Fortunately, or unfortunately, depending on your perspective, the northern boys would hang around The Lycée Marie Curie School. These boys were interested in the girls from wherever they came. But Dinh didn't care if I was from the South or North; he quickly had his eyes set on me. I was very shy and not interested in another beau. The medical student was not a serious relationship for me. We only went out a couple of times and enjoyed going to dance, and I wasn't looking for anything more. If that, even. We were lucky to have met but were not destined to be together.

My mother was adamant about me not being interested in Dinh. He had a reputation for being "the north guy who liked to chase girls" and how could my mother accept any guy from the north? She still had hopes for the medical student.

In fact, neither mother (mine nor Dinh's) supported Dinh's efforts to gain my attention. At one point, his mother took the keys to his scooter away from him. To his credit and perseverance, he found an old bike and rode it to my house. It was not far for a scooter, but for a bike ride, it was a long way.

At one point, he got to know my younger sister who at the time was seven years old. He asked her if she liked ice cream and if she would like to go with him to get some. Of course, she was too young to go by herself so she asked me if I wanted to join her. How could I say no to my sister getting ice cream? He peddled with my sister riding on the handle-bars and me on the back fender. I was still not that interested, but what I didn't appreciate at the time was Dinh Tran's "perseverance." Once again, he colluded with my sister that whenever I was home, she was to put a pink ribbon on her window.

My parents had had enough. They enrolled me that fall into the Couvent des Oiseaux (the Convent of Birds). They did not appreciate Dinh Tran's "perseverance" either. The Couvent des Oiseaux also called Regina Mundi was also a very prestigious private Catholic School in Saigon. Ngô đình Lệ Thủy, niece of the President of Vietnam, and I were in the same class. My parents were giving it their best to keep me from that northern boy. Dinh's "perseverance" in the end "paid off." Our first date was a scooter ride around Saigon. Slowly, I came around to falling for him, and after I graduated from high school, my heart belonged to him.

My mother was still not convinced that this would work out. She decided to test his mother. If I really liked him and wanted to marry him, she asked me to tell his mother to come to her to ask for my hand in marriage. What's more, after marriage, Dinh and I would live with her (my mother). It was absolutely not the norm to move into the wife's family house; it should have been the other way around. But my mother was smart and was trying to save me from a life of being looked down upon and being treated like a servant. She knew that if I moved into Dinh's family home, they would always see me as the lower-class southern girl. My mother was having none of that for her child. To everyone's surprise, Dinh's mother agreed.

We dated for about three years when my mother said it was time to get married. We did. Dinh was in his third year of college, and I in my second. I became pregnant that first year. My mother took care of all the engagement plans including the engagement party. The engagement party was traditionally as important as the wedding. Without the engagement party, there would be no wedding. The groom's family took care of the wedding. The groom gave to the bride a wedding ring as well a pair of earrings to be worn at the ceremony. This gift was the official announcement. Madame Caubet, the blonde lady in front, was the Principal of the Lycee Marie Curie. She seldom attended any of her student's events. We were so honored that she attended our wedding reception.

Dung continues to care for our family even as it grew. Dinh completed college but decided teaching was not going to lead him to his fame or fortune so applied for and was accepted to Law School. My college continued but at a slower pace as I was now a young mother. Most of my friends were Southerners. Their families had no idea about the communists. The Communists then sent troops to South Vietnam. As the communist party grew, Mother lost her coffee/tea plantation to them. We were at the plantation one night when a loud crash and yelling broke into the house. The noise and mayhem awoke us to a gang of Viet Minh trying to take over our home. There were five of them, and several of them had been employed by mother to work on the plantation. She had provided for their livelihood, and now they were threatening to take hers away. They had a large roll of heavy rope, and they told her if she didn't hand it over, they would kidnap her kids, tie them up, and send them to Russia. Her first priority always was to protect her children, and that night we lost our beloved plantation.

My mother's resiliency only grew after that horrible night. She began to build the new building for the American troops. Our building was built with seven stories and a terrace on the top floor with a view of our beautiful home, Saigon. We lived on the ground floor, and the six upper floors were leased to the American GIs. Dinh helped my mother manage the rental leases.

At that point, South Vietnam instituted the draft, and Dinh was drafted into the army. They shaved his head and gave him army uniforms. He was lucky because his father still had connections with both the Army and the Police. Although it was very rarely done, they released him from the army and assigned him to the police so he could stay in Saigon. He was able to join the police force in lieu of the army.

In 1964, my first child, Tam (Tama), was born. That was the year that Dinh had been drafted. He spent one week in training before joining the police. He was able to stay in Saigon the entire time. My second child, Nhan (Ty), was born in 1967. The third, Le (Lee), came in 1971, and my baby girl, Thu (Justine) came in 1972.

More American troops came during this period. The borders were closed. Dinh helped my mother to manage the leases to American GIs. I worked in a French Pharmaceutical Lab "Roussel" specializing in the wholesale production of all kinds of drugs. It was not easy to get a job at Roussel Laboratories; you had to be very fluent in French and had to have good credentials. Luckily, my father knew everyone in Saigon because he was President of "The Cercle Sportif Saigonais," one of the prestigious sporting club for well-known people. Wanting to have an even better lifestyle, working as a side job, I went in billiard ball business by myself.

My father owned a big Department Store supplying all kinds of sporting goods in the center of Saigon. With his referrals, I got the address of Klein manufacturer of the billiard balls from Paris, France. I ordered those balls and soon began to supply to all the local pool halls in Saigon.

We made a lot of money at that time, at least a 500 percent profit because we had a monopoly in the distribution of billiard balls from France. I was a hard worker like my mom. Out of work, but not out of time! And I never felt unsafe during those turbulent years. My childhood was one of safety and security. I'm not sure I even thought about how special my mother was until years later.

CHAPTER TWO

The Waiting Game

CU CHI TUNNELS

Communist forces began digging a network of tunnels under the jungle terrain of South Vietnam in the late 1940s, during their war of independence from French colonial authority. Tunnels were often dug by hand, only a short distance at a time. As the United States increasingly escalated its military presence in Vietnam in support of a non-Communist regime in South Vietnam beginning in the early 1960s, North Vietnamese and Viet Cong troops (as Communist supporters in South Vietnam were known) gradually expanded the tunnels. At its peak during the Vietnam War (https://www.history.com/topics/vietnam-war) the network of tunnels in the Cu Chi district linked VC support bases over a distance of some 250 kilometers, from the outskirts of Saigon all the way to the Cambodian Border. In addition to providing underground shelter, the Cu Chi tunnels served a key role during combat operations, including as a base for Communist attacks against nearby Saigon. VC soldiers lurking in the tunnels set numerous booby traps for U.S. and South Vietnamese infantrymen, planting trip wires that would set off grenades or overturn boxes of scorpions or poisonous snakes onto the heads of enemy troops. To combat these guerrilla tactics, U.S. forces would eventually train some soldiers to *function as so-called "tunnel rats." These soldiers (usually of small stature) would spend hours navigating the cramped, dark tunnels to detect booby traps and scout enemy troops. (History.com/topics/Vietnam-war/cu-chi-tunnels)*

By 1975, the migration from the north had escalated. Dung realized it was time to sell the building that had housed American troops and was now filling up with Northern refugees who had fled the north. The attacks on the city became ongoing, and chaos and uncertainty were becoming the norm.

Fighting had escalated from Guerilla warfare to out and out battles between North Vietnam and parts of South Vietnam. We had heard about what was happening but pretty much led normal lives except for American soldiers arriving every day. Then the war was at our doorstep.

The fall of Saigon, also known as the "Liberation of Saigon," was moving more rapidly than any of us, including the Americans had thought. The United States Army intelligence had predicted that we would at least last through 1976, but the North Vietnamese army was moving more and more aggressively southward. The Politburo of North Vietnam (PAVN) demanded "unremitting vigor in the attack all the way to the heart of Saigon."

And quickly it moved. On April 9, the Army of the Republic of Vietnam (the ground forces of South Vietnam) set up the last line of defense in Xuan Loc; they held ground for eleven days before finally withdrawing. The Army then organized five centers of resistance to defend the city, but as the exodus from the city ramped up, many of those leaderless soldiers left the battlefield and joined the march.

As we followed the news each day, we knew our lives were getting more in danger. Having fled communism from the North once, Dinh knew that we had to leave. On April 21, President Nguyễn văn Thiệu resigned in a tearful televised announcement, blaming the Americans for the failure to aid South Vietnam. The North Vietnamese were just twenty-six miles outside of Saigon.

On April 29, Saigon was hit by PAVN rockets, and forces fought their way to the outskirts of the city. It was happening so fast. On April 29th, General Dương văn Minh received orders from the Politburo "to strike with the greatest determination into the enemy's final lair." Also, on April 29th, the South Vietnamese Air Force began departing from Tân sơn Nhứt Air Base signifying complete loss of the Air Force.

By this time, we had received word from France that the urgency was eminent. I had a girlfriend who I worked with in the Lab whose mother was living in France. The mother had sent her news asking her "to leave immediately." She and her family went to the airport Tân sơn Nhứt, but before she left, she had two Samsonite suitcases filled with jewelry; she trusted me and wanted me to keep one for her in case something happened to her. I could give back to her later on when we arrived safely in United States. She waited for three days at the airport before she was able to get a flight out. Despite the curfew, Dinh and I made sure that I got her suitcase back to her before she left, and at that point, she gave me as a souvenir a beautiful emerald and diamond set of earrings, ring, and brooch. We all understood our need to take action.

We packed what we could as quickly as we could. We took with us a little food, a box of noodles, and a bag of pork jerky. We had a single toothbrush for all of us. In an army bag, we filled Vietnamese money (piasters) which we were able to exchange for American dollars, thanks to a policeman who worked for Dinh. He also owned a jewelry store located right in the district of the Harbor Police where Dinh worked. He was able to exchange at the last minute the piasters for gold leaves. I had taken a jacket that I cut slits into and stuffed with gold leaves. With an old maternity blouse and all the treasures in my coat, I looked like I was expecting a child.

Vietnamese Piasters (*below*)

We left for the boat dock on April 29 around noon. By then, bombing had started all around us. We had planned on just taking the immediate family, but Dinh also needed to take his father, mother, siblings, and their children. We had about twenty people with us. There was also a neighbor who Dinh knew if he stayed, he would certainly have been killed. He had worked undercover against the Communists.

Thanks to Dinh's connection with the police (he was the Chief of the Harbor Police by then), we had a police escort through the streets of Saigon which enabled us to break curfew. We arrived at the docks which were loaded with people trying to get on boats. We got to the cargo boat that Dinh had been able to secure through his connections as Chief of the Harbor Police. With the affidavit that Dinh had provided through his connection with the Harbor Police, the boat was allowed to stay docked until we all arrived. When the captain saw all the additional people we had with us, the captain ordered we could only take the seven of us who had been planned and would pay for passage. By now we were a crowd of forty-five. There was a lengthy heated argument about including everyone as well as charging for them, but when Dinh threatened through his authority as a Police Chief, to open all the gates that were holding back most of Saigon, the captain agreed. He knew that if those gates would have been opened, a stampede of scared, determined families would have rushed his boat. Dinh paid the agreed upon price of one leaf of gold for each traveler. (In April of 1975, the exact value of each bar of gold was $200/a wrapper with 12,057 ounces of thin gold leaves.)

In the early hours of April 30, General Duong van Minh received orders to fully attack. The result is history.

Once the boat was loaded, it quietly and slowly left the harbor to the safety of open water. As dawn arrived and we were safe, the bombardment of Saigon escalated, and by the end of the day, the city had fallen to the Communists.

> "I, General Dương văn Minh, President of the Saigon Administration, appeal to the armed forces of the Republic of Vietnam to lay down their arms and surrender unconditionally to the forces of the Liberation Army of South Vietnam. Furthermore, I declare Saigon government completely dissolved at all levels. From the central government to the local governments must be handed over to the Provisional Revolutionary Government of the Republic of South Vietnam." 11:30 a.m., April 30, 1975

> **Lieutenant Colonel Bùi văn Tùng announced on the radio,** "We, the representatives of the forces of the Liberation Army of South Vietnam, solemnly declare that the city of Saigon was completely liberated. We accept the unconditional surrender of General Dương văn Minh, the President of the Saigon Administration. The Vietnam War is over." 2:30 p.m., April 30, 1975.

Our boat, the Dong Nai, was a large cargo ship. It was our passageway to the free world. We were fortunate to have a cabin below. It was small and dark. Most of the passengers slept on the deck in rows. We all shared several upper deck bathrooms. There was a pregnant lady with us who needed to use the bathroom frequently, and at night, she had to step over all the other sleeping passengers on her many trips to the "head." My brother-in-law complained that he couldn't get any sleep because she kept waking him up by walking across his body. We were given one bowl of rice each day, and the only water we had was when we stopped for supplies. Needless to say, we went through our box of noodles and pork jerky very quickly. Our days grew longer and longer, and boredom was our continual companion. We would go out to the deck and watch the dolphins swim by the boat. We also heard on the radio that our Vietnamese piasters would be of no value once we got to America. We had converted some of them to American dollars, but we still had many more left. So, to pass the time, we made little paper boats, filled each with a few worthless piasters, and let them go into the ocean to ride alongside the dolphins. It helped to pass the time. Our journey lasted nineteen days.

My youngest daughter was only two for her first "boat ride." Shortly after we started, she broke out in a rash across her throat and neck. We had no water for bathing, and in the heat and cramped quarters, the rash became more and more inflamed. She was still in diapers. She cried and cried. My mother and I took turns caring for her. It was during that time she discovered that inserting her two front fingers in her mouth to suck on would in fact make her feel better. That soon became a habit hard to break. Looking back on it, I smile in that *her* daughter did the same in times of stress or boredom. Must have something to do with genetics. Occasionally, the boat stopped for supplies. Members of the crew and some of the male passengers who could speak English boarded other American ships for juice and water. With these new supplies, we were able to have fresh drinking water.

I continued to wear my jacket of gold leaves, and as such, I did have my own challenges with skin discomfort. It was so itchy. The captain continued to complain about not paying for the extra travelers and eventually took Dinh's gun away from him for spite if nothing else. We arrived at the Philippines, Subic Bay on May 19th. Subic Bay is a bay on the west coast of the island of Luson in the Philippines, about 100 kilometers (sixty-two miles) northwest of Manila Bay. An extension of the South China Sea, its shores were formerly the site of a major Navy facility. The U.S. Naval Base was to be our home for the next two months. Tents had been set up for twenty to thirty people, and plenty of food was available for us. Outhouses had been built to meet our toilet needs. It was a smelly experience. We all took turns dumping those latrines up in the mountains. All except Dinh. For whatever the reason, he was so lucky never scheduled for the task. Several people noted they couldn't eat for several days after they had that assignment. Most days lingered on as we were waiting for sponsors to be identified who would be our resource for assimilation in the States. We spent most of our time watching over our luggage and carry-ons as they held all our belongings as well as gold, money, and jewelry. They were our future. Whenever the family went to the barracks for meals, one person always stayed back to watch over the items. Dinh's mother made the mistake of talking about where Dinh's big brother kept his bag. The conversation was overheard. That night when everyone was asleep, the man who had overheard the conversation, slipped over to where the bag was laying, quietly grabbed it, and ran out of the tent. He had made the most of the opportunity before him. The next morning, it was discovered that the bag was missing, but as no one had seen it happen, no one could identify the thief. Tension mounted in the tent.

Fortunately, a small boy needed to use the outhouse, and when he got there, there was a man "sitting on the throne" counting the money with the stolen bag beside him. The thief had thought the best place "out of sight" was in the outhouse. It never occurred to him that a little boy might unexpectedly show up and see what he was doing. When the little boy saw the man counting the money from the bag, he knew what he was witnessing. He ran back and told his mother what he had seen. When Dinh heard the news, he approached the man and told him to give everything back. He assured the thief that if he ever went back to Vietnam, he would be arrested. Dinh explained to the man that he was the Chief of Police in Saigon, and his father was a judge. There would be little to discuss. He would certainly have been arrested and thrown into jail. The bag was quickly and completely returned.

I had a close call myself. I had my bag with me as I went through the buffet line one day, and as it was hard to manage the bag while serving myself, I set the bag down as I plated up. I forgot about it until I got to the table. Once I realized what I had done, I was overcome with shock and panic. Fortunately, no one noticed it as they had gone through the line. Like me, they were focused on their meal. Whew. That would have been a tough message to deliver to my husband.

Other than being there during the rainy season and we were stuck inside most days, the sun would break through finally, and we could take the kids to the beautiful beach to frolic and play in the sun. The American GIs were friendly and seemed to enjoy the children. There was one in particular who was a giant of a man. He was always pleasant to Dinh and me. My daughter was getting more and more attached to her finger sucking routine, and even though we tried everything we could think of to get her to stop—from hot ointment to lotion, to tying her hand down—she remained insistent that this was a necessary habit for her well-being. We asked our friendly giant if he could help us out. We told her that if she didn't stop sucking her fingers, that "giant" was going to take her away. The next day while everyone was playing beside the water, she began to suck on her fingers. Our friendly giant witnessed it from afar and quickly leaped in the air and ran for her yelling "AAAAARRRRGGGGHHHHH." She immediately withdrew her fingers from her mouth and never sucked on them again. Every parent needs a friendly giant of their own for disciplinary purposes.

I am proud to say we were neither afraid nor anxious about our future. Dinh and I talked about taking cooking classes, so when we arrived in the United States, we could start a catering business. We were sure that our Vietnamese professional credentials would not translate to the American job market so we were preparing for our future if nowhere else but in our dreams. We lived each day with the certainty that whatever came our way, we would manage as a family. We knew two of the four children would be ready for school as soon as we arrived which would make for a quicker transition for them. The two little ones would probably not even remember much about their homeland. We were content to wait. Our wait began to pay off as after two months, we took a plane to Guam, and the next day, we arrived at Fort Chaffee, Arkansas. Dinh's family would end their journey in Pomona, California. It would be years before we would see them again.

We settled into Ft. Chaffee for our next period of waiting. Ft. Chaffee is Arkansas' National Guard facility and has been serving the community since 1804. We were housed in base barracks. Families were separated by army blankets that were hung across wires to serve as walls. There was one exception to the "wall effectiveness." There was a guy there with two wives.

Even though each wife had their own "living rooms," they still could not agree on anything. We could hear them arguing over who was going to wash clothes that day and who was going to make dinner. The arguing was endless, and the blankets served no purpose as a noise barrier.

We were so well fed that many of the women and girls used the milk for facials. We had never seen so much milk. Together, we learned US culture through the eyes of Hollywood. Movie night was popular for all of us. We learned Hollywood humor through Charlie Chaplin. And nobody was funnier than Lucy and Desi. We loved to watch movies starring by James Dean such as *Giant* and *Rebel Without a Cause*. John Wayne was another favorite.

We were proficient in both Vietnamese and French, and though we spoke a little English, we knew we were going to have to gain a greater English proficiency in speaking as well as writing so we attended English lessons regularly. We made our barrack's house of army-blanket walls into *our home*. We knew we would have to wait longer than other families because there were more of us. With four children and my mother, a family of seven would take longer to find a sponsor. We patiently waited.

CHAPTER THREE

New Home, New Land

*"Everywhere immigrants have enriched
and strengthened the fabric of American life."*
–President John Kennedy.

"More than any other nation on Earth, America has constantly drawn strength and spirit from wave after wave of immigrants. In each generation, they have proved to be the most restless, the most adventurous, the most industrious of people. Bearing different memories, honoring different heritages, they have strengthened our economy, enriched our culture, renewed our promise of freedom and opportunity for all."
–President Bill Clinton

"VIETNAMESE IMMIGRANTS IN THE UNITED STATES"

The arrival of 125,000 Vietnamese refugees to the United States in 1975 was among the most dramatic evacuations undertaken by the U.S. Government, matched only recently by the chaotic flights from Afghanistan following the U.S. military's withdrawal. This initial group of Vietnamese immigrants was followed by more refugees and their families, and the Vietnamese foreign-born population in the United States roughly doubled every decade between 1980 and 2000.

The 1.4 million Vietnamese immigrants now in the country represent one of the largest foreign-born groups in the United States and account for about 3 percent of the overall 44.5 million U.S. immigrants as of 2019. The Vietnamese immigrant population is the fourth largest Asian immigrant group in the United States after those from India, China, (including Hong Kong) and the Philippines.

Within the United States, 52 percent of all Vietnamese immigrants live in either California or Texas. After their initial adjustment, they tend to have higher incomes, are less likely to be in poverty, and more likely to be insured. (*www.migrationpolicy.org/article/vietnamese-immigrants-united-states.*)

The day finally arrived when we got word that a sponsor had been found, and we could make our last steps of the journey to our new home. The United Kavanaugh Methodist Church in Greenville, Texas would be our sponsors. Greenville is located fifty miles NE of Dallas and is the county seat of Hunt County. The United Kavanaugh Methodist Church was named after Bishop Hubbard Hinde Kavanaugh, who had been a leader in American Methodism. One of the tenants of the church states, "We believe the Christian Faith is best lived in community." These words certainly rang true for the support and care we were given. Rev. Dan Shaw and his wife Betsy and Dr. Truett Crim and his wife Margaret met us at the airport in Dallas, upon our arrival to our new home.

Dr Truett Crim and wife Margaret

Driving from Dallas to Greenville, reality set in. We found ourselves homesick for our homeland; we were scared of how we were ever going to build a successful and productive life in Texas. Would we ever be able to communicate effectively enough to thrive? How will our children do in the new schools? Would they be able to make friends or would they be considered "strange" and "different"? Where and how would we live?

Our worries were needless. When we arrived at our new house, a big house on the property next to the church, the members brought over a banquet of food for us—fresh fruit, meat, vegetables, and plenty of sweet treats for our children. The members were so excited that we had arrived that their excitement made us immediately feel welcomed and cared for.

Dinh found a job at the local store, Gibson's, (much like a Walmart) as a custodian. It was not the job of a Police Chief, but it gave us time to figure out the lay of the land. I asked if I could go back to school to get my certification as a pharmacist, but the school was in Galveston, and I could not leave my family. So, our routine set in. We were given a large clothing donation from the church. Betsy dropped off and picked up the children from school every day. Tama was eleven; Nhan (Ty), eight; Le, four; and Thu, two and a half. Thu stayed home with my mother until she was old enough to start school. The church embraced their new Vietnamese family; the children made friends and quickly adapted to their new environment.

One afternoon, Margaret took me to the only Chinese grocery store in downtown Dallas. There I got a supply of fish sauce, rice, and noodles. When I got home, I looked at the bottle of fish sauce and found the manufacturer's contact information for this product. It was clear that Dinh could not continue at his $2.50 @ hour job, and we needed a new plan.

I contacted the fish sauce manufacturer in Hong Kong, and they gave me the number in California that might be interested in doing business with us. I called them and found out what I needed to get started. I knew I wanted to open a grocery store in Dallas. My sponsor asked me why Dallas and I replied, "Why not?" They could not believe how quickly we were able to begin a new business. And I had seen some Catholic Vietnamese refugees attending mass at the St Pius Church in East Dallas so I knew there would be customers available for our store. We came to Greenville, TX in September 1975 and tried our new adventure six months later. We leased a very small building in East Dallas in the neighborhood we wanted; it happened to be close to the St Pius church. We built shelves, and a member of the Methodist church gave us a very old cash register. We were starting to look like a grocery store. We only sold fish sauce, rice, and noodles. Few months later, we added canned goods to our inventory. We now had water chestnuts, bamboo shoots, and mushrooms to name a few.

We were the first ones to open a Vietnamese food store for our people in Dallas. We named it Tan Viet Market. Tan Viet meaning "a Vietnamese market in a new country."

It was a crazy adventure to open up a grocery store without knowing how big Dallas–Ft. Worth was. For six months, we drove back and forth every day from Greenville to Dallas to our little store, driving an old Rambler that had been given to us by the church. Leaving early in the morning and going home in the dark for six months, we were so tired that we decided to move to Dallas leasing a small house in the neighborhood in East Dallas. We had been in Greenville for six months. Dr. Crim and his wife Margaret (we called them Marnie and Papa Crim) loved us to death and worried how we can handle our business without getting loans from the bank. They let us borrow $5,000 without signing any documents, and with that support (equivalent to $30,000 in today's market), we saved it so we had money to grow.

Business began to boom. We could never have done it without the love and support from the Methodist Church, Rev. and Mrs. Shaw, and dearest sponsors, Dr. and Mrs. Crim. Our business continued to grow, and we quickly needed a larger building. It was almost impossible to get anyone to agree to give us a lease as we had no past record of financial stability. Dr. Crim gave us a recommendation and assured them that he would cover the cost if needed. We were able to get a building across the street from the old one which was part of a strip mall that included several other Vietnamese restaurants, salons, and stores. We had 2,500 square feet to fill. We also had a section of fabrics at the store.

[Photos (*top down*): Our grocery store, we added fabrics due to demand, Dragon Dance for New Year, family business]

Running a limited grocery store is hard work and made us very little money. We realized we spent too much time for very little money. We knew we had to expand our inventory once again. We added more food choices that included meat and fabrics. I also appreciated the need within the community for medicine and medical supplies.

Life back in our homeland was a very different story. The losing side of any civil war is devastating. The North knew they had to quickly deter any of the south's hope to regroup and regain their country back. Soldiers were ordered to register and report for "reform and retraining" camps. These were not the Nazi style of death camps, but they did impose brutal discipline and hard labor. The soldiers were never sure they would ever be free again. The land which had been rich and productive was now barren as a result of the American's continued bombing raids. Land reform was not successful, and there were widespread food shortages. The results of the war created an enormous humanitarian crisis. These were our friends left behind and families struggling. We decided we wanted to be the humanitarian "relief" to this crisis.

In 1982, we contacted our relatives left behind in Saigon. We began to understand the needs and urgency of helping these families. We stocked our shelves with fabric for clothing and food that was shippable. We also shipped radio cassettes and became the first distributor of JVC in Dallas. And we knew there was a medicine and medical supply shortage.

With my background in pharmaceuticals and my old diploma, we were approved to handle medicine. As we were still buying from California, our costs were so high that we still didn't make much profit. It was then I realized we needed to get into the wholesale market. I did my homework and understood we needed a license for that. We applied in Austin for a wholesale license for shipping only and were approved. We got our medicine directly from Dallas and were able to set up a pharmacy within our store. We also needed to provide shipments of antibiotics (erythromycin and chloramphenicol) to Vietnam. People in Vietnam were struggling to get supplies.

> **TEXAS DEPARTMENT OF HEALTH**
>
> **WHOLESALE DRUG REGISTRATION**
>
> ESTABLISHMENT REG. NO. 057-1063
>
> TAN-VIET DUOC CUOC
> 10315-21 Ferguson
> Dallas, Texas 75228
>
> The above registrant has paid the required fee of Twenty-five Dollars ($25) and is authorized to engage in the wholesale distribution of drugs for the fiscal year ending August 31, 1983, pursuant to Article 4476-5, Texas Civil Statutes, Texas Food, Drug and Cosmetic Act.
>
> Receipt No. 0328
> Date August 31, 1982
>
> Robert Bernstein, M.D., Commissioner
>
> MUST BE DISPLAYED AT ABOVE ADDRESS
> Non-Transferable

Our business was booming so much; we were attracting customers not only from the city of Dallas but also from those living in surrounding counties like Kaufman, Sulphur Springs, Tyler Commerce, and Rockwall.

The Vietnamese living in and surrounding Dallas would come to us with a list of supplies their families back home needed. We were able to become the hub of resources to send back home to the families in need. We packaged up boxes with all that was requested and shipped them back to Vietnam. We had our boxes ready by early afternoon to be sure they were picked up by Air France to be shipped to Vietnam. We were now meeting the needs of the community, of our families back in Vietnam, as well as creating a better business model. We did advertising for our people living in the Dallas–Ft. Worth area saying, "Lá lành đùm lá rách" "Healthy leaves cover broken leaves." In other words, the good leaves protect the worn-out leaves. People help those in need. We put a big sign in front of our store. We had a Western Union machine in our store so we could send telegrams directly to their relatives. We provided food, cloth, medicine as well as the ability for our customers to wire money through Western Union to their friends and relatives. We provided one-stop shopping for our customers to support their families back home. We were exclusive in this now booming business. As the older generation of customers retired, the next generation became our customers. They still call me respectfully, Mrs. Tan Viet. We were so proud to have helped our people in Vietnam. After ten years of apogee, our business slowed down with the competition of some pharmacies in Vietnam ordering direct from Hong Kong.

We had to add a section of bridal gowns and beautiful designed pieces of fabric to make our traditional Áo dài.

We also had a video section at the store (renting Hong Kong movies dubbing in Vietnamese). At that time, the Kung Fu movies were so popular and very profitable. We loved to watch *Anh Hùng Xạ Điêu* (*The Legend of the Condor Heroes*) and *Thần Điêu Đại Hiệp* (*The Return of the Condor Heroes*). We were so abducted by those series of Kung Fu movies. We could not sleep by watching nonstop.

In 1995, real estate was booming. Dinh became a licensed Real Estate Agent working with Century 21. We started to buy condominiums and houses on foreclosure and leased them to Asian immigrants.

For the next twenty years, the store became our life. We continued to add new items as demand required. We cut other items that had become unpopular. We were in tune to the pulse of the community and responded as needed. All of our children worked every afternoon after school to help with the business, and today, they are all successful businesspeople. They all attended Southern Methodist University. My mother stayed at home and took care of the household as well and providing us with delicious home-cooked Vietnamese meals. As the children discovered the difficulty of American teachers and school workers to pronounce Vietnamese names, one by one, they converted their Vietnamese names to more American and easier to pronounce ones. Tam became simply "Tama,"

Nhan answered to "Ty," Le adjusted to more easily recognizable American name "Lee," and when it came time for our baby (the infamous finger sucker) Thu, with the help of our sponsors, became "Justine." I became "Lily" and Dinh morphed into "Dino"—rhymes with "Casino"—one of his favorite "playgrounds."

And then, a most unexpected event happened.

CHAPTER FOUR

Starting Over

It was a normal Saturday morning. We were all working in the store, taking care of customers, moving inventory, enjoying the day, when at 11 a.m., we began to smell smoke. We looked for the source and saw smoke coming from the electric box. There had been a shortage in the box, and smoke was billowing out. Lee ran next door to the pharmacy to get another fire extinguisher, but quickly, the smoke turned into angry flames, and there was nothing we could do but call the fire department. They tried to save the building by opening a hole in the roof, and even with water everywhere, there was nothing we could do but watch it burn. We lost everything that fateful morning.

The only thing that was saved even though it was drenched was the fabric we sold. When the insurance came to measure it for the reimbursement value, it would not even roll out to be measured. They ended up weighing it to estimate its value. We were closed for six months. We had nothing left. All the hard work and building a new life for ourselves and our family was gone. We were going to have to start all over with nothing but new ideas and dreams. Staying at home and doing nothing was just not our style. At that time, Nail Salons were becoming very popular. As I had nothing else to do, I decided to go to Cosmetology School and learn how to become a nail technician and to get my license to practice. Dinh began to look around for a new location.

The grocery store never opened again as a grocery store. We rebuilt what we could, hung shelves, and turned it into a Block Buster Store. Ty had just graduated from college with a teaching degree, but after one year in the classroom, he decided teaching was not for him. He took over and ran the video store. With much creativity, he built it up even more. Knowing how much kids loved movies and video games, he worked out a deal where the kids would run around town, posting flyers about weekly deals, and new releases; he paid his young workforce with free rentals. Business soared.

This was the time that satellite television was a growing industry. Through his experience running the video store and with his dad's business acumen and advice, the business bloomed. Lee started working with Prime Star Satellite but decided to go into the Home Theater business. Ty liked the Prime Star opportunities so did both the video store as well as starting new opportunities with Prime Star Satellite. He did the upfront work and hired others for the installation. They both found successful careers in their individual paths. Through the years, business boomed.

Since we were never going to re-open our grocery store, I had completed my schooling and was once again ready to take on a new career. Dinh found the perfect location for a nail salon at the SE corner of Preston and Beltline in Dallas. We soon opened a five-chair salon. The location was perfect as it was a busy high-end neighborhood surrounded by shopping centers. We quickly hired more technicians and filled all five pedicure chairs. We were called Simply Nails.

Our technicians were all young Vietnamese girls who spoke very little English. They were bright and eager to learn, and many of them have their own salons today. One young girl in particular didn't know the English word for "foot." (A pretty critical word needed to give a pedicure.) She didn't know how to say, "Ma'am, please put your foot in the water."

There was a gentleman she respected who was a good customer, and so she felt safe asking him if he would give her the English translation. Thinking that he was quiet a comedian, he told her the English word was "pussy." When the next lady came in and sat down at her chair, she removed the customer's footwear, and calmly and assuredly said, "Ma'am, would you please put your pussy in the water?" The wise-guy broke into hysterical laughter as did everyone else around who had overheard her. It was received by all in good humor. This young technician now owns her own salon in Houston.

As the salon grew everyday, I knew expansion was always the key to success and decided it was time to get into the skin care business.

I was sixty years old at the time. Dinh was a natural business manager and leader, so I knew as I could spend my time doing research while he ran the business end.

I went back to the Cosmetology School for skin care and for an additional license. Eight months later, I had my own space in the back of the salon where I did eyebrow waxing. At first, it was offered as a free service and quickly grew into a profitable new service. I then added facials at 50 percent off offering the standard line of skin care. Again, quickly I was able to charge a standard industry rate. We were now Lily Day Spa.

But I was hungry for more. I knew that the real profits were in the selling of the products to our clients from the nail salon. I did some research. I went to many different skin care shows. Luckily, I had a friend who worked for the Aloe Vera company. This company sold to different skin care providers because aloe vera is an essential product in quality and effective skin care. I continued doing research by going to different companies and looking for the best sellers. At that time, Alpha - Lipoic Acid from Dr Perricone was very popular.

I took classes with Dr Fulton, American dermatologist and researcher, who co-invented Retin-A, a popular acne medication. I slowly connected with different labs and created my own line starting first with five products using a combination of the most innovative formulas of the esthetic and medical advances at that time such as the Alpha-Lipoic Acid, Glycolic, Vitamin C, and Copper Peptide that were the best sellers in the business.

Later, we have created the Lily Dermaceuticals, a comprehensive array of rejuvenating products for all skin types of skin care. Our line was meticulously formulated to be safe and beneficial, using super-refined ingredients, to deliver the most effective skin care available. They were customized to intensively treat the premature signs of aging for home use as well for professional estheticians.

We opened the Lily Dermaceuticals Website with our trademark. Cosmetic folks don't have to go through FDA with only lotions, cleansers, and other potions.

The nail salon had grown with ten chairs called Lily Day Spa, and again, it was time to expand. There was a large empty building adjacent to our salon that created a new opportunity for us. We leased the building and divided in twenty-three rooms. We had massage parlors, hair salons, and additional nail salon. Each room was leased out to individual owner of each specialty. We called it Les Salons de Beaute'. We saved two rooms for me and my daughter Tama to sell the Lily Dermaceuticals products. We also offered education and training with our customized clinical products to others Vietnamese nail salon owners willing to expand their business in the skin care industry.

Our older daughter Tama had spent twenty years as an American Flight Attendant. As our business grew, her curiosity and natural creativity toward this venture also blossomed.

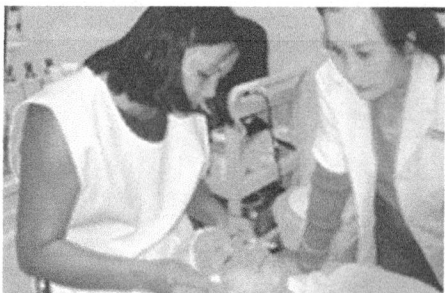

We also offered training classes to young estheticians willing to expand their business in the skin care industry.

CHAPTER FIVE

Heartache

I was sixty-one years old. Life was running on the fast track. My day used to be busy from the start to the very end. I began training new classes of providers of skin care and lotions. My children were all busy starting their careers and marriages. And yet, I began to suspect... Dinh's behavior was becoming more and more erratic as he was constantly away from me and our business. I figured it was just Dinh being a "nice guy" and helping others when needed. Back when we had the old grocery store, a customer started shopping with us and became a "regular." She was married and had three daughters; she was a nail tech, working at another salon so at that time we didn't have a lot in common, but they invited us to dinner on occasion, and back then, I had eligible sons we thought perhaps they were hoping for a future son-in-law. One of the daughters had tried very hard to get the attention of one of our boys, but the age difference was too great—he was eighteen and she fifteen. I told my son to run away as fast as he could; that there could be serious repercussions for him if anything romantic ever happened. He heard me and distanced himself.

After the fire at the grocery store, she urged us to open our own nail salon. She helped as we set up our new business; she cleaned an and helped get us ready. Time passed, and after our salon opened, she thought this would be her "in" to Dinh's attention. And then they rented one of our condos. She would call Dinh asking for help with repairs around the house. Again, it was just Dinh being nice, and he always responded to me, "Nothing will happen."

And then came the horrible trip to Lake Tahoe. They invited us to join them on a trip to Lake Tahoe. It sounded like a fun idea. However, once we all got there, Dinh and Lorie (not her real name) became inseparable. They would walk side by side on all the outings with my family and hers together. They would go off together, laugh, and tell private jokes while we all watched by the wayside.

I saw it unveil before my own eyes and could not believe what I was seeing. On Mondays, Dinh always made bank deposits. We had one bank with many different locations. I would see the receipts from banks all over town, but when I questioned him, he said that he had to drive all the way to East Dallas at the bank close to our old Oriental Market; they had better service for whatever particular service he needed that day. I still did not believe. Then we bought a beautiful home in Plano, and before I knew it, Lorie and her husband moved in just down the street. The excuses were never ending for Dinh to stop by and help her with whatever reason she could "think of." All of the Dallas Asian community knew what was going on. They would see the two of them enter restaurants, movies, shopping—among other things. They knew Dinh's car because he drove a red convertible expensive Mercedes.

He would leave for the bank in the morning and return late in the afternoon before I got home. One day, one of my family members saw him with her hands in hands. Dinh was so scared, begging him to keep secret. "Please don't tell anything, she might commit a suicide." Listening to Dinh, he did not tell me anything, but I knew that something was going on. There are no words to say how deeply it damaged my heart.

At night, I would walk the neighborhood, even in the winter by myself like a crazy woman, until I got so tired that I went home and was able to go to bed. It was so hard for me; daytime I went to work as if nothing was happening to me. Never being a woman to play the victim, I decided to hear what was happening myself and bugged and recorded all the phone conversations. At the end of the day, I could play them back and listen myself to what was happening to my marriage.

We continued to work our businesses together. My friends and family thought I should divorce him, but everything I had was joined together with him. How could I break up with the success of our shared life? Yes, there were days that we fought in our salon. When we argued, we argued in French. Of course, everyone in the building knew we were fighting. You don't need to understand the words to know by the tone and volume of the voice; it was obvious we were not deciding on where to go for dinner.

I was so distraught, I decided to cut off all my hair. I cut it as short as a pair of shears could cut. I thought him seeing this would trigger his guilt for driving me to such a horrific and self-deprecating act that it would bring him back to me. He only told me how awful I looked. I became more and more devastated. My children never said anything to him and didn't want to interfere; they just asked me to divorce him.

I was not the only victim of this affair. My mother cried every day. While she and Dinh had had a rocky start together, over the years, they had become quite close. When we were living in Saigon, the building that my mother owned, after the American soldiers left, was rented out to the northern Vietnamese who had escaped Communism. Most of them did not have the credentials to be there. Because Dinh's Dad still had influence and because Dinh was the Chief of Police, they could each look the other way and allow for the families to stay. It was a tremendous help to my mother.

Life brought mother and Dinh closer together, and as we came to America, the bond became stronger and stronger. But with all that was happening to her daughter, mother cried all the time privately. However, when Dinh was around, she acted as if nothing was wrong. Together, we cooked for him, washed his clothes, and provided a beautiful home for him to find comfort in. She did not want to make the case worse.

Privately, she would say, "Lily, there is more than one man in the world, you are so stupid, why not leave him?" Even one of my American girl friends from the Cosmetology school told me that I was so weak, so naïve, I needed to take vacation, go on a cruise, or Happy Hours on weekend. One day I listened to her and tried a glass of red wine at home first because I never had experience of drinking. I got drunk right away, felt on the floor, and broke my pinky finger.

Again, how could I remain financially successful if I did go through a divorce. How could I find a job since I was self-employed for twenty-five years in Dallas. I was so busy to take care of my clients, and I had to have someone at the front desk. He knew that all my children had their own world and nobody could help me. He kept sneaking day time to have lunch with her and stayed night time at home.

Finally, I couldn't live with this anymore. Living on and off with a man who disrespected me for almost ten years. I couldn't control our income. Dinh came to the store and sneaked out almost everyday to go to see her with the pretext that he was going to the bank. I was so tired; I cried every night while continuing this never-ending life. All my children told me to divorce him. I couldn't do that because I was so ashamed; I always honored him in front of our friends acting like nothing was happening. It was so hard on me. I didn't deserve what he was doing to me. He forgot all the sacrifices that I did to raise our children; he forgot how hard it was for me to marry him when I was so young, still in college with no income.

I finally figured out a way to end this. Once at 2 a.m., I called Lorie's husband. I had invented a reason for him to come over. When he arrived, I told him that I thought his wife was having an affair. Both Dinh and I knew this man owned a gun. Dinh heard me tell him about his wife, and knowing about the gun, he got very frightened. (I never said who the affair was with. I just knew that it wouldn't take long to know Dinh was the "other" guy. Dinh realized the same.) I could see Dinh turning pale. I set up a lunch date with the husband telling him that I would help him find a Private Investigator to look into the matter. Once he found out who it was, he could then give a warning to the "other guy." But a warning only. He was not to use his gun. I wanted the affair to end; I did not want to end my husband's life.

I then wrote a letter to Dinh. In it I told him that I was so tired. That I was working so hard each day and for so long and that I didn't deserve to be treated this way. I told him to do whatever he wanted, but that I needed to know. He said he needed a month to think. I told him if he chose me, the affair would have to end.

I bought a ticket to Paris heading for Lourdes. I left a note with my mother, but she was the only one who knew. I took the train to Lourdes that night and became very frightened as a strange man kept staring at me the whole time. Fortunately, I made it there safely the next day and was glad to get off that train. When I got to Lourdes, I prayed and prayed. I asked God why I deserved something so awful. And then I looked around and saw so many other people so less fortunate than I. My prayers changed from "Lord, get me out of this mess," to "Lord, give me the peace to handle whatever is your will."

I returned to Dallas with a whole different mindset. I reminded Dinh that he had to give me an answer soon. And he did, he said he would quit seeing her. And I believe he did. Trust is a hard thing to lose and then gain back. It didn't happen overnight. It wasn't easy at first to believe him, but over time, it became easier and easier. He was always where he said he would be; we worked together side by side, and gradually, a very fragile trust emerged. Lorie got divorced and had many more affairs with different men.

On January 14, 2014, Dinh and I celebrated our fiftieth wedding anniversary. Surrounded by friends and family, our union, while not the pure unblemished union as before, had survived what to many was un-survivable; we settled into a new kind of love and friendship. Forgiveness had been given but one can never forget. We worked at building our life back together one day at a time.

[50th Anniversary Party Photo]

We were no longer the girl from south Vietnam being sought after by the handsome dashing boy from the north. Long gone was the young family working hand in hand to build a future in a war-torn country only to escape in the night with bombs dropping all around us. Those scared yet determined kids in love who built not one, but several successful businesses were but a memory. We were a couple with infidelity and heartbreak in our relationship. And still, we were willing to try to find our love and commitment once again. And yet, our biggest struggle of "life" was still ahead of us.

Six months later, Dinh was diagnosed with cancer. For the first year, we cherished each day doing all the things he loved. Working, dancing, a little gambling here and there, and precious time with his children and grandchildren.

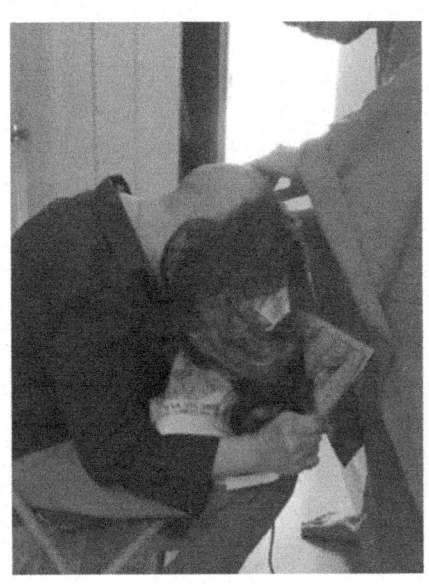

[Photo: I shaved my hair to support Dinh]

As the cancer ravaged his body, the family surrounded him with all our love. We supported him, cared for him, and encouraged him. As his hair began to fall out from the chemo, I went to the Buddhist Monk and had my head shaved. It was the second time my hair was part of my journey. Tama had completed her master's degree in nursing by then and was able to help us understand what was happening. We each took turns holding him, making him smile, and helping him to find comfort.

Before he died, Dinh asked for a Priest. He wanted the Last Rites and wanted to profess that Jesus Christ was his Lord and Savior. The local priest could not be found, but a visiting priest from Vietnam came and offered the ritual and received Dinh's profession. Dinh made his final journey Home an hour later. A new kind of heartbreak overtook my soul.

CHAPTER SIX

The Love of My Life

DINH'S EULOGY BY CHAZ POKORSKI

Thank you, everyone, for being here today. I know your support means a lot to the family, and Dinh is looking down at everyone and smiling. My name is Chaz Pokorski; I am Dinh's son-in-law, married to his daughter Justine (or Thu).

Dinh Tran passed peacefully with his friends and family at his side. I'd like to say a special thanks to Mr. Hong and Mrs. Cindi who were with us on that dark day. It was very important to Dinh to convert to Catholicism, and he and the family will ever be indebted to you guys for making it happen and for all the arrangements thereafter.

Obviously, each of us here have a different relationship with Dinh or Dino. . . or as I call him, Bo. When I first met him, he was in his classic black dress slacks, button-down shirt, Mont Blanc pens, Rolex. . . he was dressed to the nines that day. . . and, has turned out, pretty much every day thereafter. He welcomed me as he did most, with a smile and compliment. I was totally at ease being with him. He had style. He had class. . . at first, I wondered if he was that way to me just to keep an eye on me as I was dating his daughter, but he was that way with everyone he met.

[Photo: Guardian Angels]

Come also to find out, that unassuming, easy-going guy who looked the part out of *GQ (style)* magazine, Saigon, was one of eight children born, grandson to district governor in North Vietnam, and son to a former Chief Justice of the Supreme Court in South Vietnam. . . I didn't really know what those titles meant for all these years. . . but digging into them at bit further, I found out a district governor is loosely equivalent to a mayor of a major city in the United States. . . and then when I looked up his dad's title, Chief Justice of the Supreme Court, I was like WOW! Turns out that title translated to a role similar to that of an attorney general. . . and I have to admit, deep down, I always wondered if he was secretly Vietnamese mafia, but as it turned out, he was actually Vietnamese royalty (or at least to me). So Jonathan, Isabella, Audrey, and MaxiLu—it's not just your good looks you get from Ong Noi or Ong Ngoai, turns out you were dealt a pretty good hand in the smarts department as well!

Royalty or not, Dino's family was forced to move to Saigon when he was fourteen years old. The family was uprooted and determined to start over—a thread that would prove over and over again throughout his life. Luckily, in Saigon, however, he found another constant thread in his life, one that was MUCH better! Lily Trieu caught his eye one day, and he courted her on his motorcycle. I am sure he tried to impress her with his French—he attended a French high school which was apparently a pretty prestigious thing at the time. . . problem was, Lily also attended another French high school in town—so it was on to plan B. Now most of you probably already know this, but Lily is by far the best negotiator I have ever seen. I went to school for it, read case studies about the best. . . no one would have a chance against Lily. . . So courting her, wow, I can't imagine the hoops poor Dinh had to jump through to get her attention. The way I figure (after the motorcycle and the French failed), either Lily's negotiation skills had not yet fully developed, that or she, like other daughter in South Vietnam, thought dating a boy from the North would be the best way to torture her father. Either way, Lily and Dinh were married in 1964 while Lily was in Pharmaceutical School. Their marriage was the first nonarranged marriage in both families. They had four children together, and there are still pictures of the family on that same fateful motorcycle. . .

Given that his father's profession, it was expected that his children would go on to law school. But two years prior to graduation, he was drafted in the Army. Given a choice of the army vs. acceptance into the police academy, he chose the police academy. He graduated a captain and eventually went on to be Major in the Saigon Harbor. Now my brother-in-law Greggy and I had to work for it, lots of cognac and even balut (hot vit lon, i.e. fertilized duck egg boiled), but when he finally told stories of what his life was like as a Major in the Harbor, I had images of him hanging out on the patio of Bistro B, cigarette in one hand, cold beer in the other, hanging out with the GIs and his buddies—he was respected and enjoyed the life with his friends. I bet it was pretty awesome, and he mentioned how much he enjoyed that chapter of his life.

He moved to South Vietnam from the North, he got settled, had a family and a career, but like so many other families in Vietnam in the seventies, his family too was forced to fight for their future. In 1975, Dinh made arrangements to have his immediate family board a boat and flee Vietnam.

Problem was, when it came time to board, there were way more passengers than were originally negotiated (I couldn't imagine having to pick which aunts, uncles, or cousins to include). While I would normally have all my money on Lily in ANY negotiation, as I understood it, the owners of the boat pulled out guns, "no one is getting on". . . and then, like a classic Western movie. . . with the sunset as the backdrop, silhouettes of John Wayne/Dinh's boys from the police department appeared over the horizon, guns drawn. In the end, Dinh's boys outnumbered the boys on the boat. An agreement was made, and Dinh and his family (numbering nearly forty-five people) boarded the boat. . . and as cool and Wild West as it sounds years later, it's most likely a reflection of Dinh's kindness and generosity that his friends were again there for him in his time of need.

The family went to Guam, California, and eventually settled in with a kind family in Greenville, TX in 1976. There, the son of an Attorney General was bagging groceries in a Gibson's (like a Walmart) in East Texas. How humbling it must have been! He did it though. He loved his family and he did it for his family. . . the good news though was that Dinh was also smart enough to pick an awesome wife. Not sure it is widely known that Vietnamese women not only run the home but also typically have all the business smarts. Mrs. Cindi of course knows this, but Lily, probably managing the way Dinh was bagging groceries (maybe mixing cleaning suppliers with vegetables).

She was smart enough to identify a distributor on the back of a bottle of fish sauce. Lily and Dinh, with the help of their dear sponsor family, and the distributor from California, opened up the first Vietnamese grocery store in Dallas. . . and it's crazy, years later, I am still out to dinner with the family, and folks will stop by and shake Dinh's hand. I can't imagine what it would be like to be so far removed from my family and loved ones. . . And it was their store that was the vehicle that connected those families to the other side of the world. There, people could send letters, money, and even medicine to loved ones in Vietnam. . .

I think it's also worth noting. . . so we all grew up listening to our parents tell us they had to walk twenty miles, uphill, in the snow, to get to school every day (each way). . . well, apparently, child labor laws being what they were in North Texas in the eighties—now Dino's children get to add to the existing narrative. . . they get to say, when I was your age, I worked in my parents grocery store. Tam—I had to carry fifty pounds bags of rice. . . and I only weighted fifty pounds. Justine—I had to pick crabs out of the aquarium and not get pinched. . . I feel bad for the grandchildren! This chapter too would come to an end. After several successful years running the store, there was a fire and the store was no more. Dinh (and Lily) would have to figure out their next chapter. Again, he was reminded of how smart he was to marry the love of his life. Together, they targeted the salon industry and opened up a nail salon. Obviously, this is most of our recent memories of him I think it's worth noting, however, that this occurred when his kids were in college. The kids had an opportunity to see their parents' courage to start their own businesses, which I am sure played a role in Ty, Le, and Tama's entrepreneurial spirit that eventually lead each of them to start their own successful businesses. . . Justine, you apparently were too Americanized and ended up working in corporate America! But I know he was proud of his children and their ability to provide for their families.

Once the kids got busy with their kids and things slowed down—Dinh and Lily had a chance to re-kindle their love story, spend more time together, and specifically spend more time together dancing. For the past few years, he truly loved being out dancing. He danced with old friends like he used to when he first came to the United States. He made new friends, young friends who embraced him and in turn made him feel young. . . and he danced with his beloved wife. There were days near the end when he may have only gotten out of bed a few times in a given week, but he would find the strength to make it out on a Saturday night to be with his friends; I am sure he would want you all to know how important you were to him.

... so I wasn't sure how I was going to end the eulogy, but I kind of thought I would sum up his life for how I would want my daughter to remember him and of the time we spent together.

- He loved his wife and he loved his family

- He was generous and kind, and he went out of his way to help others in need.

- He had style. He looked equally stylish at work, as he did at the casino, or at the dance club.

- ... and he had charisma—people enjoyed being around him; young people, old people, people of every race and nationality.

- But one thing that may not be as apparent upon first impression... Though he was not an intimidating 6'5", 220 lbs, he was an absolutely tenacious fighter. To start over as many times as he was forced to, to each time answer the call with resolve and determination. I see it in his stories over time, and I witnessed it first hand at all the doctor's appointments. In a time where many think the world owes them something, his story is one that shows that nothing is ever given, you have to work hard and fight. And he did that until the very end.

Bo, we'll miss you.
We love you.
May you rest in peace.

In Memoriam

Dinh Tran
1940 - 2016

LILY H. TRIEU

CHAPTER SEVEN

Continuing the Legacy: The Next Generation

LILY MED SPA AESTHETICS AND LASER CENTER – BY TAMA TRAN LISEMBY

As my grandmother had taught my mother the value of hard work, perseverance, and the necessity for resiliency and rising to life's challenges, so did our parents, Dinh and Lily teach us. I was born into a world of privilege and comfort. As the war took its toll on our lives, I learned from them—escaping in the dark of night from the bombing of our homes, sleeping on the deck of a cargo ship, eating new strange food, hours of boredom waiting, just waiting, to arriving in a strange land—were merely the challenges of each new day. We adapted.

When we finally arrived in Greenville, TX, my reality seemed bleak. I was eleven years old. I had grown up in a beautiful Saigon, a bustling city with all the amenities of a cultured civilization. As we pulled into the parking lot of the United Methodist Kavanaugh Church on that fall afternoon,

I thought I had landed in a land barren of anything beautiful. It was out in, what seemed to me, the "middle of nowhere," devoid of sunshine, color, or scenery. The leaves were all brown, the day was dark, and the smells were unusual. To this day, I dislike the smell of Doritos. Central Texas was certainly not the tropical paradise I had grown up in.

My disappointment was short lived, however, when we were met by our new sponsors and the other members of the congregation. They appeared to be truly excited about our arrival and welcomed us with plenty of good food and fellowship. I was quickly enrolled in school and, because of the limited proficiency in the English language, was put in the second grade. In my old "private school," I had been in fifth grade. My time in second grade lasted a week, third grade was another week, and I skipped fourth grade, and within the month, I was back in fifth. Apparently, my time in my old school had paid off, and I acclimated quickly.

Like all of us, we worked in the grocery store every afternoon after school. Justine ran the cash register at an early age. I was expected to lift fifty-pound bags of rice even though I barely weighed fifty pounds myself, and the boys worked the stock room. Once the video store opened, they gravitated to that end of the business.

I attended SMU as did all of us kids and spent twenty years as a flight attendant with American Airlines. As I watched my parents move from the grocery business to the nail salon, and as I gained more seniority with the airlines, several factors came into play. I had time on my hands. I was also needing a new calling in life. I needed to have a purpose, to help people, and to challenge my brain and expand my knowledge.

They had just opened Les Salons de Beaute as an extension of the nail salon, and I took over two tiny rooms to grow my skin care profession. I was still flying but very seldom, and even when I flew, I had "down time" on many flights (I flew international flights) and was able to find the time to do more studying.

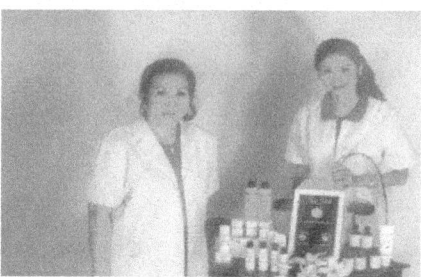

I first earned my Associate Degree from El Central College in Dallas. Within two years, I completed the program, passed the Boards, and became a Registered Nurse. I continued working in my two little spa rooms, did occasional flying, and then was accepted to the University of Texas, Arlington, TX. Two years later, I earned a Bachelor of Science Degree in Nursing.

I had considered working in a hospital and was invited for an interview for an internship at the Ft. Worth Health Resources. It was a big deal to have been invited for the interview, but the selection was very limited, and I didn't get the offer. I think "life" had other plans for me.

While I had stayed on the "cutting edge" of the industry all the while I was occasionally flying, how this business was moving! Botox was a new product, photo facials were seldom done, and the whole industry was changing. I had bought several new in innovative pieces of equipment, and while the costs were exorbitant, I knew the future was there, and I wanted to be ready. During this time, I was also fortunate to have fallen in love and married "my guy." As a newlywed and a new business owner, I not only had the great love of my life but also had my very own personal attorney. Believe me, if you could convince an attorney that these equipment purchases were a good investment, you knew you were on the right track. He was not always easy to convince so I built up my debating skills to a new and higher lever. He has supported me all along the way.

I knew it was time for three things to happen. I had to retire from flying; I had to move out of my two-room incubator; and I wanted a Master's Degree. I completed my Master of Science in Nursing from Maryville University, St. Louis, Missouri and became Board Certified in 2017. We moved to our current location, and today Lily's Med Spa is one of Dallas' top five spas. As quoted in the *D magazine*, "Our secret to success is to provide the best possible care with reasonable pricing while listening and responding to patients' needs and desires. Aesthetics should work together like an orchestra. With the right treatment, age is just a number."

I have been fortunate to be able to train doctors and nurses on injectables, and I enjoy connecting with the community through volunteering with DIFFA, North Texas Food Bank and Genesis Women's Shelter.

I attribute my success as a human being, a businesswoman, and a wife, to both of my parents. From my dad, I got his great sense of intuition. Both He and I are able to understand and truly enjoy people. We can work through most situations, keeping the peace and dignity of those with whom we work. From my mother, I have the same gift that she got from her mother. Nobody can roll up their sleeves and get to work—and work harder—than us. I include my kid sister and brothers with the same drive.

Ty, Le, and I traveled our journeys to success through the beginnings of our parent's business ventures. My sister, Justine, certainly got her work ethic and quality customer service values from those early years at that little cash register, but her professional life took its own path in the corporate world. There may still be times in her intense pressure-cooker of the workplace to re-insert those two little fingers for a little calm and soothing, but at this point in her life, she has found other more professional techniques. Nothing like a relaxing pedicure at an upscale nail salon.

Tama Tran

OWNER, LILY MED SPA

TAMA TRAN WORKS AS A NURSE PRACTITIONER AT Lily Med Spa, but her interest in skin rejuvenation began as a child working alongside her mother at her small aesthetics shop. Tran became passionate about bridging the gap between beauty and health and opened Lily Med Spa on a shoestring budget in a two-room office. Word about Tran's gorgeous results quickly spread, and she moved to a larger North Dallas location offering comprehensive skin rejuvenation treatments that restore healthy skin and promote a more youthful appearance. If it's proven and effective, Lily Med Spa excels at it and is among the top injectors in the U.S. "Our secret to success is to provide the best possible care with reasonable pricing while listening and responding to patients' needs and desires," Tran says. "I understand the value of self-care and utilize my experience in blending science, medicine and technology. Lily Med Spa is the fruition of my dream." Tran understands balance and harmony of the face. "Proportion is important," she says. "Aesthetics should work together, like an orchestra. With the right treatments, age is just a number." Tran also trains doctors and nurses on injectables and contributes to promoting the "look good/feel good connection" throughout the community, often volunteering for causes where she can make a measurable impact, such as DIFFA, North Texas Food Bank, and Genesis Women's Shelter.

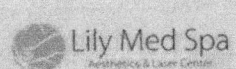

972.503.5459
lilymedspa.com

D Magazine, September 2022

CHAPTER EIGHT

My Family

TY TRAN

Ty was such a great help to us and the business when he was a teenager. The movie business grew and grew because of him. He stayed with us as we grew, and he was the last to leave the family business. He wanted to make sure our business was secure. At Dinh's funeral, Ty spoke of all the business lessons he learned from his Dad.

Ty saw the satellite industry as a new and upcoming opportunity for him to use his background and knowledge gained from our family business. He soon found his own way to great success. He became a rising star in the distribution of satellites and has won many awards for four years in a row.

He is married to Van Anh, also a hard worker and innovator. She has been very supportive of their successes, and they work well together. The have accumulated many rental properties in office buildings. They were very excited to build country homes for lease in Athens.

    They have a wonderful son Jonathan who also excels in the academics. He will be attending college next Fall 2023. Where else? SMU as is the family tradition. SMU Southern Methodist University located in Dallas has been called the Harvard of the South. SMU has been ranked one of the best universities in the nation by various publications, including *U.S. News*, *Forbes*, and *Times Higher Education*. My grandson Jonathan was accepted at SMU with a full scholarship. He is so sweet and a humble hard worker like his dad. This family works hard and plays hard. They love to travel and have seen many faraway places around the world.

LE TRAN

What family would be complete without a member who lives his life within his own norms and standards? As noted in the English expression, "He is a man who answers to the beat of his own drum." Le is the man whose creativity, charm, drive, and loyalty are "his own."

When we were trying to expand the grocery store, videos were becoming popular. We could get Korean action videos that became top sellers (renters) in our store. Le understood the power and popularity of this new addition and created his own marketing tool to increase business. He and his brother got the local boys to go around town spreading posters for the upcoming new videos, and they paid for them with free rentals. Win/Win for everyone. This grew into satellite TV, and Le stepped into that new business world. He has grown it into a very prosperous home theater business with all the bells and whistles. As new and innovative ways to enjoy this pastime developed, he grew with it. He can even work with the senior generation to teach them how to master their newly installed equipment. His ability to think "outside the box" and creatively use the resources available at the time as well as anticipating the resources that would soon be part of the industry, ensured his success.

It is in his charm, his intelligence, and his way of seeing the world with a clear understanding of what "is" and not what people "would like it to be." He is the guy who will say what everyone in the room is thinking but is afraid to say. He sees the emperor without any clothes and will tell you exactly what he looks like. Words are never curbed. He walks into a room and a gust of fresh air comes in with him. His eyes always sparkle.

Le has blessed me with two beautiful granddaughters, Isabella and Audrey. They each carry with them, their father's sense of "unique individuality." Annoying, loveable, kind, exasperating, intelligent, rough, always in a hurry, and the biggest heart in the room. Every family should have one.

"JUSTINI" (THROUGH THE EYES OF HER HUSBAND)

Not many people get to marry the girl of their dreams, but in my case, I was one of the lucky ones. I first met Thu "Justine" Tran during the height of the telecom boom in Dallas. Expense accounts created a social scene that brought the industry to some of the nicest restaurants and sporting events in town each night. For those who lived through it, you knew exactly where the Motorola seats were during the Stars games, the Texas Instrument seats during the Mavericks games, and ultimately wind up in a packed Old No. 7 club when either team played. You'd come across sales representatives from NEC at Primos for happy hour, only to meet up with different colleagues from Intel at Sipangos later that night. If there wasn't a game, it would be just as likely that you spend an evening out having dinner and eventually dancing to Emerald City (back when they played at venues in town).

Justine worked in sales for a semiconductor distributor. First blush, she carried herself as any other Texan. She dressed like a Texan, she drank margaritas like a Texan, and she even had a Texas drawl when she spoke. The industry was competitive, but it felt more like a fraternity for the people who worked in it. Everyone knew everyone, and it wasn't long before friends set us up. We officially dated a few months after we met. It may have been a few more months after that when I was introduced to her family.

We were out on the town with friends when Justine received a call that her beloved grandmother was in critical condition at the hospital with an aortic aneurysm. We rushed to the hospital where her parents were in the waiting room. While the room was somber, I was impressed by how welcoming her parents were to me. Justine's grandmother was never released from the hospital and passed away a few days later. Justine's grandmother was my first glimpse into her family's story as a Vietnamese immigrant in the United States. I later found out that she shared a bedroom with her grandmother growing up. She learned how to speak Vietnamese from her grandmother, and even today, we go out to Vietnamese restaurants, and she orders for our family in her native tongue... but even that is a small piece of her story.

Justine's family moved to the United States when she was two years old. Before she was old enough to go to school, she worked at her family's grocery store. The family worked there seven days a week and had dinner together every night in the back of the store. Justine's siblings talk about how big the bags of rice they carried, what life was like working the seafood section, or how one could make a few extra bucks selling bootleg DVDs. Justine ultimately worked as a cashier when she was old enough to do so. Whether all the adventures are true, there is no doubt that the experience gave her the work ethic she has today, an appreciation of what it means to be a family, and ironically the ability to quickly do the math on any sale at Neiman's.

While I love being a Texan, I presume diversity was not celebrated back in the eighties the same way it is celebrated today. My take is that this is probably where Justine's parents' story ended and where her story began. My take is that she probably lived two lives, one with her family and her culture and the other trying to fit in with the other kids who looked different than her.

Justine was an excellent student in high school (finished third in her class) and was eventually accepted and attended Southern Methodist University in Dallas. My impression was that she was again surrounded by students who did not look like her or come from her background, though it sounded like she was able to integrate as well as any other American living life on campus. She belonged to a sorority (delta gamma) and made friends who we still come across today. Justine graduated with two degrees (Sociology and French) and eventually took a job with a semiconductor distributor supporting the telecom industry. When I met her, she was working in one of the hottest industries, collaborating with engineers on cutting-edge technology. I laughed when I later found out what her majors were, but later appreciated her ability to find a way to not only fit in but to take an opportunity and achieve the highest degree of success. Justine was awarded President's Club that year at her company, which recognizes the top sales performers in the organization. Looking back, it was the first time I appreciated her ability to adapt, survive, and thrive, but it wouldn't be the last.

After several months of dating, I received a job offer to move to Boston. Not knowing she'd soon be my wife, Justine decided she'd sell her house, quit a job she loved, leave a family that loved her, and picked up to move to Boston. Looking back, I'm am pretty sure she knew we'd be married (even if I did not), and she was smart enough to wait for Spring in Boston before making the move. The experience was the adventure of a lifetime, and I'll always remember her parents coming to visit. We had a one-bedroom brownstone in the Back Bay that would be considered pretty nice by most standards, but when her parents saw our place, there was a long discussion in Vietnamese before Justine said to me, "My family worries that you are poor!"

It wasn't long until Justine and I were engaged and moved back to Dallas. Planning for a wedding anywhere can be extravagant, expensive, maybe even overwhelming, but not for Justine. In a theme that was starting to materialize (adapt, survive, thrive), it was not enough to just get married. Justine and the family would have a wedding that would rival the likes of most Dallas elites. We were going to get married on the SMU campus and have a reception at the Mansion on Turtle Creek where legendary chef Dean Fearing would be serving the food and Emerald City would be rocking the dance floor!

Married life was great, but made even better when Justine became pregnant with our daughter Maxime Luu Pokorski. Maxime was named after the town of St. Maxime in the South of France where Justine and I spent part of her pregnancy, and where her extended family vacationed. Luu was Justine's beloved grandmother's maiden name… Before long we ended up mixing the two names as only parents do, typically as parents lose their patience when a child is misbehaving—"MaxiLu don't you dare use those scissors to cut your hair!"

They say that kids grow up too fast, but life as a parent is pretty dynamic as well. A few weeks before MaxiLu was born, we called one prominent child care learning center to see if we could get our daughter enrolled... after about five minutes of laughter, they let us know the enrollment wait list dated back several years. We missed out on that one, but it was all Justine needed before she'd be an expert at understanding the competitive landscape of the private school scene in Dallas. She would gladly embrace being the economic diversity with the likes of the Hunts, Cooks, Cubans, and other Dallas elites. By Justine's hard work (and the Grace of God), our daughter was accepted and graduated from the Lamplighter school. She would thereafter be accepted and enroll at the Greenhill school. As a parent in the schools, Justine quickly made friends by way of her authentic and self-deprecating sense of humor. She'd come to look and sound like all the other parents, take on several leadership positions within the school, all while juggling a successful professional career. Adapt, survive, and thrive!

As a parent, Justine is and remains committed to giving her daughter everything she feels she missed out on growing up. Her daughter would learn to dance, figure skate, ride horses, paly sports, go to sleep away camps, snow ski (and water ski), snorkel... and the list goes on and on. MaxiLu's parents have become professional drivers. We spend most of our free time together in a car going from activity to activity singing Taylor Swift songs.

Life continues to evolve. Justine and I continue to grow as a couple as our daughter enters her teenage years. With the new found free time comes more and more of an appreciation and love for my wife and all that she does. I am able to recognize those immigrant traits where she is able to seemingly adapt to the different landscapes of life. Whether it be the ability to integrate with other parents at school, adapt for her career, and mostly blossom into a fantastic mother and wife. I'm privileged to see the fire that drives her ambition. I love that Justine won't settle for things. She won't put boundaries around what is achievable. Justine is a great role model for her daughter and a constant reminder that I need to push myself every day to be someone worthy to call her my wife.

Epilogue

After Dinh's death, I started attending Mass at the Mother of Perpetual Help Parish. I am not sure how I would have managed after Dinh's death without my new church family. They embraced me with compassion and understanding. They gave me time to heal. And yet they also understood, one must go on with living. I took Catechism classes and was baptized in the Church after his death.

I had always loved to travel, and the members of Mother of Perpetual Help planned for many excursions to be enjoyed. I was fortunate to go with them to see the world with new eyes. Those trips were not only bonding times with my new friends; I was able to see many places I had never been. Those trips made my faith stronger and stronger.

I also was able to revisit my homeland. Of course, it triggered many happy memories of my incredible mother and my courtship and then marriage to the man of my dreams. All of my children were born there—each one our own precious miracle. It was also a land of great unrest. Communism was coming in, and the changes were threatening our life styes. The years of prosperity and opportunity were gone. We no longer had the ability to realize our dreams. Our lives, our property, and our future were at risk.

And yet, it is paradise in the richness of colors, both in the city and in the countryside. The food is a wonderful combination of French and Asian cuisine that is unmatched anywhere. Art in all its forms is both precise and graceful. And the spirit of the people remains resolved with the ability to appreciate the abundant potential of each moment.

I have become an American citizen and take pride in what this country represents. I hope that my life has balanced the wisdom and love of both worlds.

Lily's Closing Prayer

Dear Lord,

You are the God of all times, and yet for me, I came to know you late in my life. Now I know that you are the God of love and the God of hope. Your love is here and now for me. Today, I am dedicating my life to loving you and doing your will. There are times in my life that I worry about my children, but I know that they are in your hands as am I. When I am weak and make mistakes like I did when I did not follow my mother's faith that I now regret, I know that I am also in your loving hands. I know your unmerited Grace forgives me of all things because your love is always with me. I have to trust in that love. I know when I have the love of God, it is greater than anything else. Now I am so humble to belong to you. Thank you, Lord, for your loving Grace.

Amen
Lily

3 Generations of Catholics

TRIPS WITH MY CHURCH FAMILY

[Photo (clockwise): Fatima, Portugal; Lourdes, France; Gaudalupe, Mexico; St. John Neumann, Philadelphia; St. Peter's Square, Rome]

[Photo (clockwise): Basilica of our Lady Guadalupe; Montreal; Jordan River; Israel]

[Photo (clockwise): Rome; Santa Fe]

[Photo (clockwise): Poland 2019 with Father Le Thanh Quang; Duc Me La Vang, Quang Tri N.Center of Viet Nam; Cha Truong buu Diep Ca Mau S. Viet Nam]

Favorite Vietnamese Recipes

THE ORIGINS OF PHO

Phở was born in Northern Vietnam during the mid-1880s. The dish was heavily influenced by both Chinese and French cooking. Rice noodle and spices were imported from China; the French popularized the eating of red meat. In fact, it is believed that "phở" is derived from "pot au feu" a French soup. Vietnamese cooks blended the Chinese, French, and native influences to make a dish that is uniquely Vietnamese from North to South. The popularity of pho spread southward starting in 1954 when the country was divided into North and South Vietnam. As the dish moved south, cooks infused it with additional ingredients until it evolved into the version that is commonly served today.

REGIONAL PHO VARIATIONS

The origins of pho as a Northern dish that spread South explains the key differences between the Northern and Southern variations. Northern style pho tends to be simpler and is made with less ingredients. There are fewer cuts of meat, and small slices of ginger are laid on top of the soup. The pho is served without bean sprouts or herbs. Instead, it is accompanied by green chilies and lime only. Southern style pho is a complex dish made from a dozen ingredients (*http://www.phofever.com/ingredients*).

php). Bean sprouts, fresh basil, and saw herb are typically served with each bowl. As with the Northern style pho, green chilies and lime are used as condiments.

PHO IN THE UNITED STATES

Refugees fleeing Vietnam in the Spring of 1975 brought with them their hopes and dreams of a better life. They also brought their cultures and cuisine, of which pho has become the most popular among Americans. Today, there are almost 2,000 pho restaurants (http://www.phofever.com/directory.php) spread across the United States and Canada. One typically finds Southern style pho served although a few outlets also serve Northern style pho. Typical establishments sell pho, and other Vietnamese dishes like goi cuon (spring rolls) and cha gio (egg rolls) (*www.phofever.com/facts.php*).